Victorian and E...

In the late 19th and early 20th centuries, the City of York with its majestic Minster and two-thousand-year history was as popular with tourists as it is today. Detailed guide-books, such as Black's Guide to Yorkshire, were available to help visitors make the most of their stay. Black's was updated each year and included historical facts about local towns and villages, where to stay, what to see and excursions to places of interest.

This booklet combines text relating to York from Black's Guide, published in 1888, with photographs taken from postcards and 'magic lantern' projection slides owned by the Keasbury-Gordon Photograph Archive.

It is in three parts. The first is thirty photographs, most of which were taken between 1890 and 1920; the second, a detailed, visitor's guide to York and the third, a general history and description of Yorkshire. Parts two and three are reproduced from the 1888 guide-book.

The Black's Guide text and the photographs complement each other and enable us to travel back in time to visit one of Britain's most interesting, historic cities. I hope you enjoy the journey.

Andrew Gill

Clifford's Tower

The Electric Theatre, Fossgate

Gillygate

Goodramgate

A Horse Tram

Lower Petergate

The Market

The Market

Micklegate Bar

The Minster

Monk Bar

The Minster

Petergate

Monk Bar

A barge on the River Ouse

The River Ouse

The River Ouse

Market Day

St. William's College

The Station Hotel

The Railway Station

Stonegate

Stonegate

The Shambles

The Shambles

The Shambles

Saint Sampson's Square

An electric tram

Walmgate Bar

Roadworks at Bootham Bar

CITY OF YORK.

HOTELS.—*Station*, at the Central Station; Harker's *York*, St. Helen's Square; *Black Swan*, Coney Street; the *North-Eastern*, Tanner Row.

Distances.

York from London, 188 miles; Birmingham, 124; Oxford, 196; Edinburgh, 209; Newcastle, 87; Hull, 41¼; Harrogate, 18½; Scarborough, 42¾; Leeds, 25½; Manchester, 67½; Liverpool, 99.

MARKET DAY.—*Saturday*.

No city in the empire can boast of an antiquity greater or more celebrated than that of York. It can very well afford to dispense with the aid of the old monkish fables which claim as its founder a great-grandson of Æneas, and contemporary of David. There can be no doubt that Cäer Ebrauc, Cäer Effroc, Eborac, Eboracum, or Euruic (not to mention any other forms of its ancient designation), was a Brigantian town of considerable importance long before Julius Agricola (A.D. 78) took up his residence in the north of England, and began to introduce Roman luxury and civilisation. The city owes its rise into importance to the Romans. Probably Agricola made it one of his principal stations; but whether he did so or not, there are good grounds for believing that the Emperor Hadrian took up his residence here about 120. Alcuin, a native of this city, in the seventh century, speaks of its foundation by the Romans :—

> "Hanc, Romana manus, muris et turribus altam,
> Fundavit primo—
> Ut fieret ducibus secura potentia regni,
> Et decus imperii, terrorque hostilibus armis."

YORK—HISTORY OF THE CITY.

> "This city first by Roman hand was formed,
> With lofty towers and high-built walls adorned,
> To give their leaders a secure repose,
> Honour to the empire, terror to their foes."

Our space admits of only a brief outline of the HISTORY OF YORK. That history comprises many of the most important events in the national annals for sixteen centuries. Round the first rude British fortification many a fierce battle was fought, as the burial mounds that still rise on the smooth surface of the Wolds sufficiently testify. Here, when Yorkshire and England came under Roman rule, the "legio sexta victrix" had its head-quarters for 300 years. As might have been expected, the Romans have left abundant traces of themselves. Besides the wall, most of which, with the multangular tower, still remains in good preservation, there have been discovered tombs (plain and with inscriptions), statues, altars, fire-places, tiles, pipes, amphoræ, urns, bronze instruments, ornaments of gold, silver, bronze, and jet, and numerous other valuable and interesting relics. It is recorded by Roman historians that the emperor Severus died here. This was in 210. In 304, Constantius Chlorus took up his residence at York. Some historians are of opinion that his son Constantine the Great was born here; but this is doubtful. Constantine, however, was at York at the period of his father's death, and assisted at the ceremony of his deification. Under Hadrian, York had received the dignity of a *civitas*, and had been distinguished by the erection of a temple to Bellona. Under Constantine, Christian churches were erected; and, according to Gough, there was a bishop of York at the Council of Arles, in 314. When the Romans finally withdrew from Britain in 450, the Saxons landed on the invitation of the British princes, and, under Hengist, retook York from the Scots and Picts. In 524, Arthur, having signally defeated the Saxons, took possession of York without opposition, and celebrated the first Christmas ever held in Britain. We pass over the struggles between Saxons and Danes, which ensued after this period. York at first submitted to the Normans, after a brief resistance, in 1068. The next year, however, the Saxons, aided by the Danes, retook the city, putting the Norman garrison to the sword. William the Conqueror took a terrible vengeance, almost entirely depopulating the country between York and Durham—the number of human beings who perished being stated by some writers to have amounted to 100,000. The first parliament mentioned in history was held at York by Henry II. in 1160 Parliaments were held in this city, more or less regularly, during the next five hundred years. During that period York took an important part in almost all the great public transactions which are recorded in English history. Here were held friendly conventions between the kings of Scotland and England. Here was Edward III. married to the beautiful and heroic Philippa; and it was from this city that the queen, in her husband's absence, marched against the Scots, and gained the great victory of Neville's Cross. It was here that, in the reign of Henry IV., Archbishop Scroop, and his friend Lord Mowbray, raised an army for the reformation of abuses, an enterprise which ended in their being treacherously seized and put to death. When the brave Richard Plantagenet, Duke of York, fell at the battle of Wakefield, the haughty Margaret of Anjou, in the insolence of her short-lived triumph, gave the order—

> "Off with his head, and set it on York gates,
> So York may overlook the town of York."

His son Edward, having been proclaimed king at London, marched to York, where Henry VI., Margaret, and the Prince of Wales were stationed, and defeated them in the bloody battle of Towton. According to some accounts, Edward was crowned in the cathedral. The events of the next few years are too well known to require to be recounted here. They are recorded in the poetry of Shakspere, and the romance of Bulwer, as well as on the more sober page of history. Edward, when he landed in England to regain his crown, committed the deliberate act of perjury in the Minster—swearing that he only came to claim his private estates, and that he would be loyal to King Henry—which affixes to his memory a stigma which his apologists in vain try to remove. The city welcomed him cordially when he returned in triumph. Richard III. visited York after his usurpation, and was greeted with a splendid reception. Some writers affirm that he was crowned here, but there seem to be no grounds for the assertion. Three years after, Richard fell at Bosworth Field, and Henry VII. made a "progress in the north," during which he made a grand entry into York. The dissolution of the religious houses by Henry VIII. caused much discontent here, and, in the "Pilgrimage of Grace" which ensued, York was taken by the rebels, but speedily recaptured, and the ringleaders executed. This insurrection, and other disturbances, led to the institution, by king Henry, of the Council of the North, which met in this city, and continued to execute its oppressive functions till it was abolished in 1640 by the Long Parliament. In 1572 the Earl of Northumberland was beheaded here, for the abortive insurrection in favour of Mary Queen of Scots and the Roman Catholic religion. James I., while going to London to receive the English crown, visited York on his way, and was welcomed with much enthusiasm. His unfortunate son removed his court to York, when his difficulties with the Parliament were increasing. The battle-field of Marston Moor, where Charles' hopes were completely wrecked, is within sight of the city walls. York held out for the king for thirteen weeks, but was at length obliged to make an honourable capitulation. At the Revolution, the citizens officially declared for the Prince of Orange, by presenting him with an address, in which they congratulated him as the deliverer of the Protestant religion. Since that time York has ceased to have a place of much importance in history. Yet one more event, and one hardly less important than any of those which have been referred to, remained to be recorded—to York belongs the honour of being the birth-place of the British Association for the Advancement of Science, which was organized here in September 1831.

"The changes," remarks Mr. Phillips, "which York has experienced in the course of the present century have not effaced, but have much impaired, its antique and singular character. The ramparts reared over Roman walls and Roman villas open to admit Stephenson and his chariots, alike impressed with the stamp of the latest iron age; railway stations replace the abbeys and hospitals which sheltered within the walls; the castle is transformed into a jail; the Gothic bridge is gone; the very river has lost its tide; and we can hardly trace the ford or ferry by which the soldiers passed from the camp of Eboracum to enjoy the baths on the road to Calcaria.

"But nature still endures; and many of the monuments of other days remain. From the summit of Clifford's, which replaced Earl Waltheof's Tower, we trace the woody vale across which, in earlier times, the cohorts marched to Derventio. The road remains which conducted Hadrada to a bloody grave, and Edward IV. to a troubled crown; and, over all, more durable and unchangeable than Norman Tower or Roman road, the smooth and shadowy Wold, crowned by the burial-mounds of Brigantian chiefs, rises calm and cold as in primeval times."*

The city of York has given to the world not a few eminent men. We mention the principal names. The learned Alcuin was born here, probably before the middle of the eighth century. His fame as a man of learning and genius caused Charlemagne to invite him to his court, and become his pupil. Alcuin contributed much to the revival of learning under that great emperor. He is even regarded by some writers as the virtual founder of the University of Paris, his academical institutions having pioneered the way for its establishment. He died, full of honours, at the Abbey of St. Martin, at Tours, in the year 804. Guy Fawkes was born here in 1570. He was of a good family; but, having become a convert to Romanism, he served in the Spanish army in the Netherlands, and was eventually deputed to carry out the plot, which has made his name a byeword. Sir. T. Herbert, the celebrated traveller, 1606. Matthew Pool, author of "Annotations," 1624. Thomas Calvert, and his nephew James, both learned Nonconformist divines and authors, were born in this city. The former died in 1679, the latter in 1698. Beilby Porteus, bishop of London, noted both as an elegant poet and writer in divinity, was born here in 1731, and died in 1808. John Flaxman, R.A., the famous sculptor, was born in 1755, and died in 1826. George Wallis, physician and satirist, translator of the works of Sydenham, was born in 1740, and died in 1802. Godfrey Higgins, author of "The Celtic Druids," etc., was born in 1771, and died in 1833. Richard John Smith, the celebrated actor of the Adelphi, was born in 1786, and died in 1855.

York is situated at the junction of the rivers Ouse and Foss, in one of the richest and most extensive vales in England. It is a county in itself, and the see of an archbishop, and occupies a position at the point where the three Ridings of Yorkshire meet. It is nearly equidistant between London and Edinburgh, and is an important centre of railway communication. The population, according to the census of 1881, was 49,530, and the inhabited houses 12,024, being an increase, since 1871, of 5734 persons, and 1755 inhabited houses. The city returns two

* "Rivers, Mountains, and Sea-coasts of Yorkshire."

members to Parliament. Its commerce is considerable, though scarcely so great as it once was. There are some large iron-foundries, and an extensive glass-manufactory. Brewing and comb-making are extensively carried on; and among other manufactures may be mentioned glass, leather, paper-hangings, confectionary, etc. Though it seems, with its narrow streets and ancient buildings, to belong to the past, York has nevertheless much of the life and activity of the present, and seems to hold out the promise of advancing in importance and material wealth as much as it has formerly declined. It is provided with the various institutions which we expect to find in a city which still claims to be the metropolis of the north of England. Such of these as require to be noticed will be mentioned afterwards.

York Minster.

Hours of admission 9 A.M. to 5 P.M. Morning prayers 10 to 11 (Sundays 10.30 to 1); evening prayers, 4.30 (Sundays 4). Visitors are admitted to the choir, lady chapel, vestry, and chapter-house, under charge of a verger, on payment of 6d. each; to the crypt or tower by special order from the dean or canon in residence.

The venerable Bede informs us that the first building on the site of this cathedral was erected by Edwin, the first Christian king of Northumbria, who was baptized on Easter day, 627. By his orders, the little wooden oratory, hastily erected for the occasion, was replaced by an edifice of stone. The building having fallen into a state of decay, was repaired and beautified by Wilfrid, the third archbishop. The cathedral suffered much in the deadly struggles of which York was the scene in 1068; but it was rebuilt on a larger scale, about 1080, by Archbishop Thomas. Again we read of its partial destruction by fire in 1137, and of its tardy restoration in 1171. At that time Archbishop Roger rebuilt the choir in the Norman style. The commencement of the present structure, however, may be dated from 1227, when Walter de Grey erected the *south transept*. In 1260, the *north transept* was built by John le Romayne, father of the archbishop of that name. The archbishop was not behind his father in zeal; for in 1291 he laid the foundation of the *nave*, which, along with the *west front*, was completed by his successor about 1345. About the same period the *chapter-house* was erected. The choir, as built by Archbishop Roger in 1171, not harmonizing with the rest of the building, was taken down, and the first stone of the present *choir* laid by Archbishop Thoresby, July 19,

1361. The funds for this, as for the other parts of the building, were principally derived from the liberality of the archbishop, who superintended the work, and from the proceeds of "indulgences." The choir was not entirely completed till about 1400. The *central tower*, which had been erected as a bell tower about 1260, was re-cased, heightened, and changed into a lantern tower, being adorned in the Perpendicular style, to correspond with the rest of the building, in 1405. The structure was completed by the erection of the *south-west tower*, commenced in 1432, and the *north-west tower*, commenced about 1470. The cathedral was reconsecrated in 1472. We shall quote only two more dates connected with the history of York Minster—1829 and 1840—both of them memorable for destructive conflagrations. On February 2d, 1829, a madman named Jonathan Martin, having concealed himself behind the tomb of Archbishop Grenfield, after evening service, set fire to the choir. The fire not being discovered till next morning, all efforts to save the choir were unavailing. The conflagration was, however, prevented from extending farther. The whole of the beautiful tabernacle work of carved oak, the stalls, the pulpit, the organ, the roof, and the rest of the wood work of the choir, were destroyed. The damage was estimated at £65,000; which sum was soon raised by public subscription. The repairs were completed, and the Cathedral re-opened, in 1832. Again in 1840 this noble edifice suffered seriously from fire. The fire originated in the south-west tower, which it reduced to a mere shell, and then spread to the roof of the nave, which was entirely destroyed. The damage was £23,000. The restoration of the parts which were destroyed has been admirably effected. A good deal has been done within the last year or two to beautify the Cathedral both internally and externally. These improvements, we believe, are mainly due to the zeal and energy of the present Dean of York. The south transept has recently undergone a thorough restoration, under the superintendence of Mr. Street, architect. It was re-opened November 1874. The construction of a new bridge across the Ouse opposite the Cathedral, and the removal of old houses in Blake Street and adjoining streets, very much improve both the access to, and the exterior view of, this noble edifice.

It is scarcely necessary to observe that, to obtain anything like a just conception of the building as a whole, it must be leisurely viewed from all sides, as well as examined in detail in its various parts. It is to be hoped that still more may yet be done to open up the surrounding space by the removal of houses of undue proximity to the Cathedral.

Exterior.

The ground-plan of the Cathedral is a Latin cross, and the building consists of a nave with side aisles ; a transept with aisles ; a choir and aisles, with a chapel in continuation. There are, besides, a chapter-house and other buildings, in addition to the general plan, connected with the different parts of the cathedral. The length of the building, from base to base of the buttresses, is 524½ feet, and its extreme breadth is about 250 feet.*

The West Front, with which we shall begin, consists of a centre and two side divisions, corresponding with the nave and aisles. These divisions are separated by buttresses, which are richly enchased with niches and canopies in relief. The buttresses form the corners of two uniform towers that rise, massive yet graceful, at the extremity of the aisles. The elevation of the central portion commences with an elegant entrance. It is divided into two doorways by a pillar composed of three clustered columns with foliated capitals. The mouldings round this entrance are ornamented with sculpture of much delicacy and beauty. The arch is surmounted by an acutely pointed pediment. Above the door is a great window of exquisite beauty, "an unrivalled specimen," says Mr. Britton, "of the leafy tracery that marks the style of the middle of the fourteenth century." The west front is adorned with various statues (among them that of Archbishop Melton, who completed this part of the cathedral), and other sculptured ornaments.

The Nave is divided by buttresses, on both sides, into seven symmetrical divisions. The north side, however, is in a plainer style than the south. The buttresses on the south side are adorned with niches, which formerly contained statues, and are surmounted by lofty and elegant pinnacles. On the north side the buttresses have each a low pyramidal cap. Each division of the aisles has a fine window in three lights, made by mullions. The clerestory windows above correspond in number. They are of five lights, and have generally a circle or wheel in the head of the arch, with quatrefoil tracery.

* The extreme length of St. Paul's Cathedral is 500 feet, and the breadth is 350 feet. Westminster Abbey is 375 feet from east to west, and 200 from north to south.

YORK MINSTER.—WINDOW ARMORIAL.

YORK MINSTER—EXTERIOR.

The South Transept is the oldest portion of the present building, with the exception of the crypt. The usual entrance to the cathedral is by the porch in the centre of this front. The windows are narrow and acutely pointed, and the ornaments are more simple and chaste in their style than those of the nave. There is a magnificent rose window in the pediment which surmounts this front. On the west side of this transept there is an ugly building used as a *Will Office*, and on the east there are *Vestries*, which it is a marvel to every tourist of taste that the people of York should suffer to disfigure their magnificent minster.

The North Transept differs materially in style from the south. Five splendid lancet windows surmount an arcade of trefoil arches, occupying the greater part both of the width and height of this transept.

The Choir (including the *Lady Chapel*, its continuation) is built in the same style as the nave, but is of a later date, and displays the progress of Gothic architecture from the decorated to the perpendicular order. The great east window, which has been pronounced by the historian of York "the finest window in the world," has on each side of it buttresses adorned with tabernacle work, and surmounted with octagonal crocketed pinnacles. A figure, supposed to be meant for Archbishop Thoresby, who built this part of the edifice, is above the window. Beneath it is a row of heads, representing our Saviour and his twelve apostles.

The Chapter House, an octagonal building connected with the north transept, has a beautiful decorated window in each side, and massive buttresses at each angle.

The Central, or *Lantern Tower*, has on each side two perpendicular windows. Its four angles are strengthened by buttresses, terminating somewhat abruptly at the top. Its top, which is beautifully battlemented, is 213 feet high. This tower is 65 feet broad, and is said to be the most massive in England.

Interior.

The entrance on week-days is by the south transept, but those who do not enter by the great west door should pass down the nave, for the sake of the view of the entire length of the minster that is obtained from the western end. The vaulted roof, a hundred feet high, stretches in a grand vista of five hundred feet to the east window, the great clustered pillars on

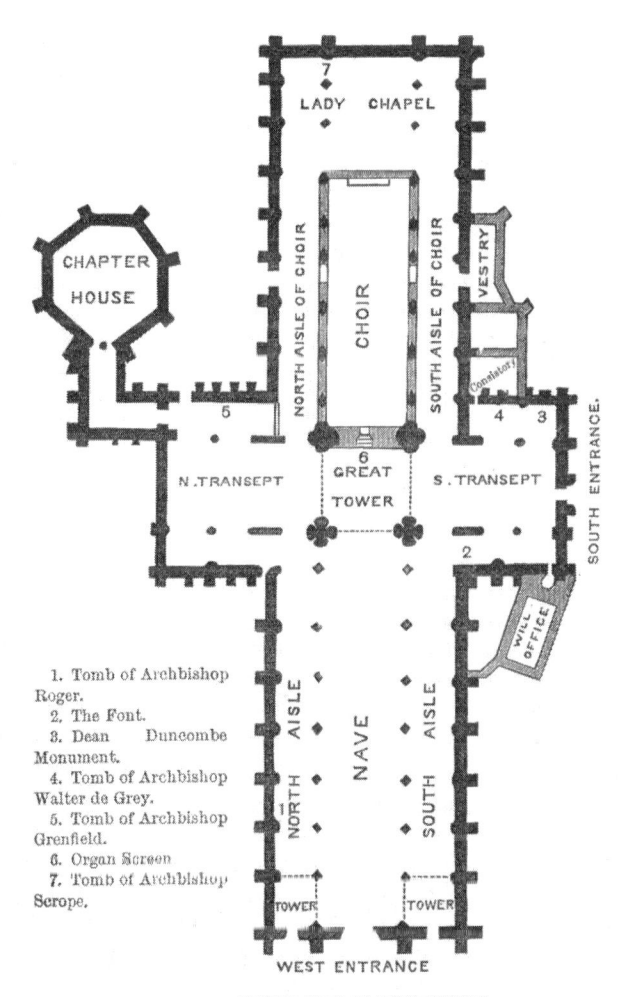

1. Tomb of Archbishop Roger.
2. The Font.
3. Dean Duncombe Monument.
4. Tomb of Archbishop Walter de Grey.
5. Tomb of Archbishop Grenfield.
6. Organ Screen
7. Tomb of Archbishop Scrope.

GROUND PLAN OF YORK MINSTER.

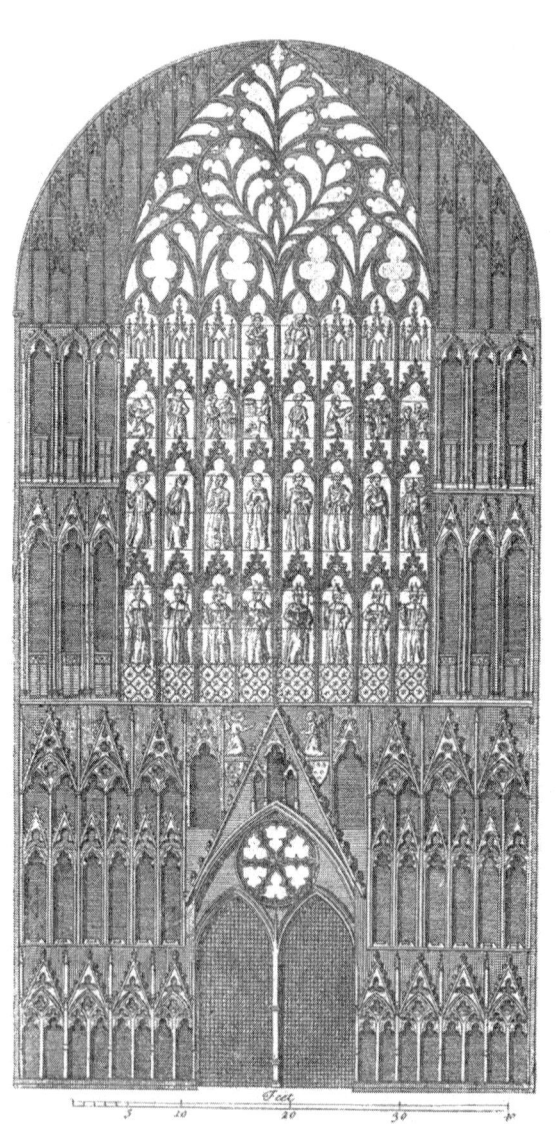

YORK MINSTER — WEST WINDOW

either side of the nave presenting a perspective which perhaps cannot be excelled in any similar building in the kingdom. The effect is greatly heightened by the mellowed light that streams down from the painted windows. The *Nave* has much interesting sculpture in the capitals of the columns, and in the ceiling. The west window, which is 54 feet high and 30 broad, is reckoned one of the finest, in the decorated style, existing in this country. The figures in the stained glass are those of archbishops of this see, along with various kings and saints. There are similar figures in the windows of the aisles. A tomb in the north aisle is ascribed to Archbishop Roger.

Coming next to the transepts, the *South Transept* is, as we have already remarked, the oldest part of the building. It is regarded as a fine specimen of the Early English style, and has lately been beautifully restored. The circular window in this part of the building is 30 feet in diameter. Beneath it are three large windows, also filled with painted glass, the figures on which are meant to represent the saints—William, Peter, Paul, and Wilfred. In the west aisle of this transept is the baptismal font, formed of dark shell marble. The east aisle possesses two tombs deserving a careful inspection. That of Archbishop Walter de Grey is extremely interesting. It consists of two tiers of trefoil arches, supported by eight columns, with capitals of luxuriant foliage, sustaining a canopy. Beneath the canopy is a recumbent figure of the archbishop. This is one of the oldest and finest tombs of this kind in the country. Walter de Grey died in 1255. Near this tomb is one ascribed to Archbishop Godfrey de Ludham or Kineton, who died in 1264. In the eastern aisle of this transept a magnificent canopied monument by Street has been erected to the late dean, Dr. Duncombe. Beneath the canopy is a recumbent effigy in white marble. The great *Central Tower* is supported by four pointed arches 109 feet high, each side having two beautiful Perpendicular windows. The *North Transept* has a series of beautiful lancet windows in its front, called the Five Sisters. The east aisle contains the altar-tomb of Archbishop Grenfield (d. 1315). A recess behind this tomb afforded a hiding place to Jonathan Martin.

The archbishop's effigy is engraved in brass, with one exception the earliest brass of an ecclesiastic in the kingdom. Here also is an altar-tomb to Stephen Beckwith, M.D. (d. 1843), who left bequests to charitable purposes amounting to £46,600. The west aisle contains another fine altar-tomb in white marble to the memory of the late Archbishop Harcourt, who died in 1847. The figure of the archbishop is recumbent, with his hands folded over a bible lying on his breast. It was executed by Mr. Noble of London, in 1855. In this aisle is the monument of Thomas Haxey, treasurer of the cathedral, who died in 1424. It consists of the effigy of a wasted corpse wrapped in a winding-sheet, and is very properly inclosed within an iron grating to preserve it from further dilapidation.

The Organ Screen at the entrance into the choir is regarded by architects as one of the finest pieces of work of this description in the world. It is of stone, and is in the richest form of the Perpendicular style. In fifteen niches, seven on the north side and eight on the south side of the choir door, are placed statues of the kings of England, from William the Conqueror to Henry VI. The last of the series is a modern work. Above these statues is a smaller series of niches, with figures of angels playing different musical instruments. The screen is 25 feet high and 50 broad. It belongs to the end of the fifteenth or the beginning of the sixteenth century; but the name of its designer is unknown.* The *Organ*, which is placed over this screen, is one of the finest in the kingdom. It was built in 1832, to supply the place of the one destroyed by the conflagration of 1829—a donation of £3000 being given towards the expense of its construction by the late Right Hon. and Rev. John Lumley Savile, Earl of Scarborough, and Prebendary of South Newbald. It underwent extensive alterations in 1859, at a further expense of upwards of £1300. It has now four sets of manuals, each embracing from CC to G in alto—56 notes, with pedals compassing from CCC to F—30 notes; the whole consisting of 69 stops, and 4266 pipes.

The Choir is entered through a beautiful canopied recess, with iron gates. It would be impossible, in our limited space, to describe all the beauties of this, the richest part of the cathedral. There are fifty-two exquisitely carved *oak stalls*, with beautiful canopies in tabernacle-work. The *archbishop's throne*, also of oak, is covered with a lofty canopy, which is much admired. The pulpit, too, is a handsome work. The wood work of the choir is a restoration of that destroyed by fire in 1829. Among other objects of interest are a brazen eagle-stand, presented

---

* The master mason, during its erection, was William Hyndley, whose device, a *hind* lodged, is visible in the upper portion of the decorations.

YORK MINSTER.—EAST WINDOW

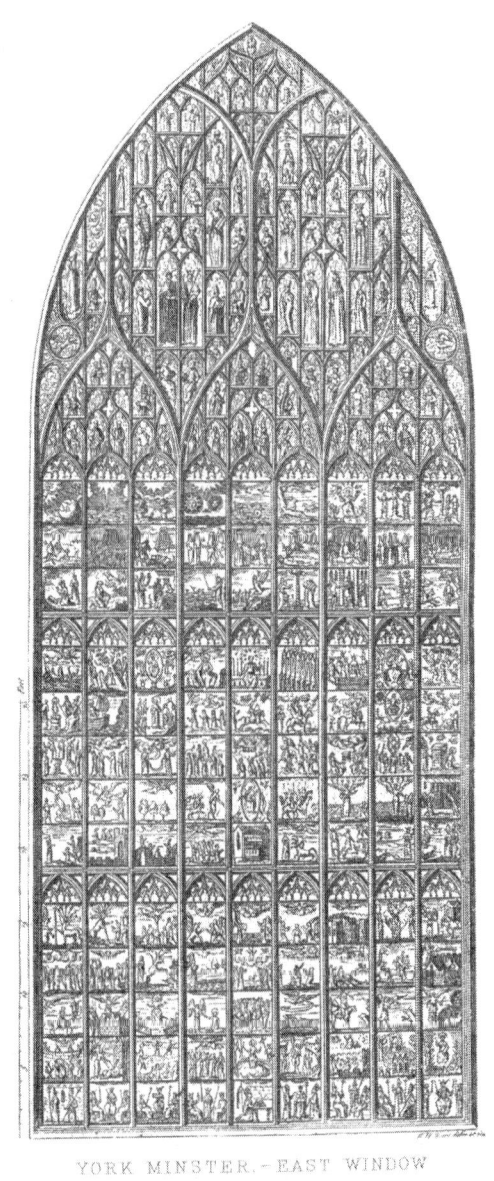

by Thomas Croft, D.D., 1686, and an *ancient chair*, said to have been used in the coronation of several Saxon kings. The *Altar Screen* is an exquisite specimen of modern workmanship, as is the *Reredos*, which has been added within the last few years. It is of oak, with figures in terra cotta representing the Crucifixion, and is so constructed as to open and shut.

The Lady Chapel extends from the altar screen to the eastern end of the cathedral. Here the attention is at once arrested by the great *East Window*, " the wonder of the world," as Drake calls it, " both for masonry and glazing." It is 75 feet high, and 32 broad. The tracery of the upper part is extremely beautiful. The stained glass of this window consists of about 200 compartments, each about a yard square, and containing figures of about two feet in height. The subjects are taken from the whole range of Scripture—those from the Apocalypse being interesting as indicating to some extent the notions prevalent at the time (1400) as to the interpretation of that book. There are several fine monuments in the Lady Chapel to archbishops of York and other persons. The monument of most historical interest in this part of the cathedral is that of Archbishop Scrope, which is under the first arch on the north side of the east window. It is an altar-tomb of freestone, covered with a slab of black marble, without inscription. Scrope is immortalised in Shakspere's *Henry IV.*:—

———— " You, lord archbishop,
Whose see is by a civil peace maintained ;
Whose beard the silver hand of peace hath touched ;
Whose learning and good letters peace hath tutored ;
Whose white investments figure innocence,
The dove and very blessed spirit of peace,—
Wherefore do you so ill translate yourself
Out of the speech of peace that bears such grace,
Into the harsh and boisterous tongue of war,
Turning your books to greaves, your ink to blood,
Your pens to lances, and your tongue divine
To a loud trumpet, and a point of war?"—*Part* II. *Act* iv. *Scene* 1.

———— " With you, lord bishop,
It is even so :—Who hath not heard it spoken
How deep you were within the books of God ?
To us, the speaker in his parliament ;
To us the imagined voice of God himself ;
The very opener and intelligencer,
Between the grace, the sanctities of heaven,
And our dull workings : O who shall believe,

YORK MINSTER—INTERIOR.

> But you misuse the reverence of your place,
> Employ the countenance and grace of Heaven,
> As a false favourite doth his prince's name,
> In deeds dishonourable?"—*Act* iv. *Scene* 2.

Scrope was beheaded in 1405. He was so beloved by the people that his grave was resorted to as a shrine. Among the other monuments deserving of notice here, are those of Archbishop Markham, under the next arch, a beautiful altar-tomb, richly carved and emblazoned with shields of arms; Archbishop Bowet, under the first arch on the north-side, a stately Gothic arch of the time of Henry VI.; Archbishop Matthew, a modern altar-tomb, erected in place of one destroyed by the fire of 1829; Archbishop Sharp, a marble monument of the Corinthian order, with his mitred effigy; Mrs. Matthew, with her kneeling figure; and Archbishop Frewen, a stately Corinthian tomb, with his full length recumbent figure in canonical robes. Most of the old effigies in the Lady Chapel and aisles of the choir are coloured after life.

The *Aisles* of the choir contain numerous monuments, many of them worthy of an attentive examination. We give a list of the most interesting. In the south aisle the following monuments are worthy of notice:—

Three monuments to officers and soldiers who fell in the service of their country: the first a handsome monumental brass to the memory of soldiers who lost their lives in the Crimea; the second a marble monument to officers and soldiers who fell in Burmah; the third, in white marble, set in black, to upwards of 500 men of the 33d Regiment who died in the Crimea.

To Sir William Gee, secretary to James I., and a member of his privy council. It is of the Corinthian order, and contains the effigies of himself, his two wives, and five children, in the attitude of prayer. He died in 1611.

To Archbishop Hutton, with his recumbent figure between two columns, surmounted by coats of arms. His three children kneel in three arches below. Archbishop Hutton died in 1605.

To Archbishop Lamplugh, who died in 1691. His mitred effigy stands on a pedestal, and bears a crozier in its hand. This monument is modern.

To Archbishop Dolben, bearing his recumbent effigy, mitred. Above is a group of cherubs, with other sculptured ornaments. This archbishop in his youth made some figure in arms. He was a standard-bearer in the royal army at the battle of Marston Moor, and was wounded afterwards in the defence of York. He died in 1686.

A monument in white marble, by Westmacott, to William Burgh, D.C.L., of York, author of a work "On the Holy Trinity," who died in 1808. It bears a full-length emblematic figure of Religion. On its base is a poetical inscription by John B. S. Morritt, Esq. of Rokeby, the friend of Sir Walter Scott.

A monument of veined marble, with Corinthian columns, to the memory of

William Wentworth, Earl of Strafford, son of the famous earl of that name. He died in 1695. The monument contains the effigies of himself and his lady.

To the Hon. Thomas Wentworth, third son of Edward, Lord Rockingham. This monument consists of a full-length statue of the deceased, erect, in a Roman habit, and with the left hand leaning upon an urn. It also bears a fine female figure in a sitting posture.

The north aisle also contains many monuments. We note those most deserving of examination, beginning at the east end of the aisle :—

A monument to Archbishop Sterne, grandfather of the author of "Tristram Shandy." His mitred figure reclines on a pedestal, the head resting on the hand. Above is an architrave, frieze, and cornice, adorned with drapery and festoons. He died in 1683.

To Sir George Saville, who was a representative of Yorkshire in five successive parliaments, and died in 1784. This monument was erected by a general subscription in the county. It bears a statue of the deceased, leaning on a pillar.

A pyramidal monument to Sir Thomas Davenport. Died 1786.

Another modern tomb to the Hon. Dorothy Langley, who died in 1824. It has a fine canopy, with pinnacles.

A monument to Vice-Admiral Medley, with bust, arms, naval implements, etc. He died in 1747.

A monument, with inscriptions, to the memory of Charles Howard, Earl of Carlisle, who died in 1684; Sir John Fenwicke, his son-in-law, who was executed for high treason in 1696; and Lady Mary Fenwicke, his daughter, and wife of Sir John. The monument was erected by Lady Mary to her father and husband. It is composed of two pilasters and a circular pediment, adorned with cherubim, coats of arms, a bust of the earl, and several urns.

A fine antique monument to Sir William Ingram and his wife, with their figures in the costume of the time of James I. Sir William died in 1623. His epitaph is worth quoting :—" Here the judge of testators lies dead in Christ, the judge and testator of the new covenant. He has given these legacies—himself to the Lord, his joys to heaven, his deeds to the world, his gains to his friends, his body to the earth. The hearts of his friends contain a better picture of his character; but, would you know his whole conduct, you must follow him to heaven."

The monument of Sir Henry Belasis and his lady. It is composed of a large canopy, supported by columns. Under it are their effigies, in the costume of the period. Below are the figures of their children.

The monument of Archbishop Savage, a fine altar-tomb, somewhat mutilated. The effigy of the archbishop lies under an arch. He died in 1507, and his tomb is regarded as a beautiful specimen of the monumental architecture of the period.

The last tomb we shall notice is that of Prince William de Hatfield, second son of Edward III., who died in the eighth year of his age. His recumbent figure, in alabaster, much defaced, with a coronet on his head, and a lion at his feet, is clad in an embroidered vest and cloak. The effigy lies under a beautiful canopy.

The Crypt (special order required) is reached by a flight of steps, descending from the aisles. This is the oldest portion of the edifice. The architecture is Norman, though not unmingled with work of a later date. The roof is groined, and supported by six Norman pillars. The excavations consequent upon the fire of 1829 led to the discovery of another crypt, extending eastward, nearly the whole length of the choir. It contains numerous interesting portions of Saxon and Norman architecture, but is seldom shewn to the visitor, owing to the dense darkness.

The Vestry adjoins the south aisle of the choir. It contains various curiosities. Chief of these is the horn of Ulphus. The tradition connected with it is, that Ulphus, a Saxon prince, to hinder his two sons from quarrelling about their inheritance, solemnly presented the whole of his lands and revenues to God and St. Peter, accompanying the gift with the ceremony of kneeling before the altar of the Cathedral, and drinking the wine with which he had filled this horn. The horn is of ivory, and is a curious and valuable relic of ancient art. Archbishop Scroop's indulgence cup, some antique silver chalices, a silver crozier, archiepiscopal rings, an old copy of the bible, with its chain attached, and other relics, are also shewn here.

The Chapter-House is on the north side of the cathedral, and is entered by a vestibule from the east aisle of the north transept. It is octagonal in shape, and is 63 feet in diameter, and 67 feet 10 inches high. Each side of the house, except that in which is the entrance, has a large and beautiful window, filled with stained glass. Much of the beauty of this building is owing to the absence of any central pillar (so often found in chapter-houses) for the support of the roof, which is of oak, beautifully groined. Forty-four stone stalls are ranged round the entire circumference, below the windows, for the dignitaries who compose the chapter. Each of these stalls has a fine projecting canopy, composed of three acute arches, crowned with canopies, and ending in finials. Above the canopies, a gallery goes round the wall on the level of the sills of the windows. The Chapter-House was carefully and tastefully restored in 1845, £3000 having been left for the purpose by Dr. Beckwith. Few who examine this beautiful building will deny that it is indeed an architectural gem, and that the inscription in Saxon characters over the entrance door has in it not a little appropriateness :

" Ut Rosa Flos Florum,
Sic est Domus ista Domorum."

(As is the rose the flower of flowers,
So of houses is this of ours.)

The Towers can now only be ascended after obtaining a special order. From the central tower the eye can sweep over an immense extent of the great vale which extends from Durham into Nottinghamshire and Lincoln. There is a fine peal of bells in the south-west tower, the bequest of Dr. Beckwith; and in the north-west tower is a monster bell, purchased by subscription (£2000), one of the largest in England. It was erected in 1845, and strikes only at noon.

The principal *Dimensions of the Minster* are as follows:—

External—Extreme length, 524½ feet; breadth (across the transepts), 250; height of central tower, 213; breadth of do., 65; height of western towers, 202; breadth of do., 32.

Internal—Extreme length, 486 feet; breadth (across the transepts), 223½. Choir—length, 223½; breadth, 99½; height, 102. Nave—length, 264; breadth, 104½; height, 99½. South transept—length, 104½; breadth, 90. North transept—length, 96½; breadth, 94½. Organ screen—height, 25; breadth, 50. Lantern tower—height, 188. East window—height, 76; breadth 32. West window—height, 54; breadth, 30. "Five sisters" —height, 54; breadth of each, 5¼. Chapter-house—height, 67; diameter, 63.

Near the Minster, on its north side, are the *Deanery*, the *Library*, and the *Residentiary*. The Deanery and Residentiary are modern. The Library was formerly a chapel of the archiepiscopal palace, part of the remains of which still stand between it and the Residentiary. The Library (open Wednesday 11 A.M. to 1 P.M., and Saturday 2 P.M. to 4 P.M.) contains some rare and valuable works, amongst which are Queen Elizabeth's Prayer-Book, with autograph, and two York Breviaries.

SAINT MARY'S ABBEY AND THE MUSEUM GARDENS (open 10 A.M. to 6 P.M. Admission 1s., cheaper terms to a party).—The Gardens of the Yorkshire Philosophical Society contain within their bounds a large assemblage of objects of interest. Undoubted Roman, Saxon, and Norman remains may here be studied and compared with each other, and with the wonderfully beautiful Early English architecture of the ruined Abbey of St. Mary. In addition to these remains, which are the chief attractions of these pleasantly laid out grounds, there is an excellent museum, containing, among its curiosities, relics of a still older date connected with the county. A few hours may be passed both pleasantly and profitably in these gardens. During the summer months a military band plays in the Gardens once a week—on which occasions they form a fashionable promenade.

ST. MARY'S ABBEY will probably first claim the attention of the tourist, when he visits the Museum Gardens. The early history of this beautiful ruin is involved in some obscurity. It appears, however, to have been founded about the year 1078, when Alan, Earl of Richmond, gave a church and four acres of land to some persecuted monks of Whitby. The church was dedicated to St. Olave. In 1088, William Rufus laid with his own hand the foundation of a larger building, which was dedicated to St. Mary. This, the original abbey, was destroyed by fire in 1137. In 1270, the abbot, Simon de Warwick, undertook to rebuild it; and he lived to see it completed, which was effected in twenty-two years. This abbey soon grew to be one of the most powerful and important in the kingdom. Its abbot had a mitre and a seat in Parliament. At the Dissolution in 1540, there were 50 monks in the establishment, and the yearly revenues were rated at £2091 : 4 : 7¼ of total income, and £1650 : 0 : 7¼ of clear value—a great sum for those days. Soon after the Dissolution, an order was issued for the erection, on a portion of its site, of a residence for the Lord President of the newly instituted Council of the North ; and accordingly the church and offices of the abbey were dismantled. The palace so built was called the *King's Manor*, and is now used as a school for the blind, and dedicated to the memory of William Wilberforce. In 1701, license was granted to the authorities to take materials from this venerable ruin to repair York Castle; and again in 1705, it was used as a quarry for the restoration of one of the city churches. At a later date, it afforded stone for the repair of Beverley Minster; and the work of demolition might have been consummated ere this, had not the Yorkshire Philosophical Society succeeded in obtaining from Government a grant of the abbey and the greater part of its site. Considerable portions of the old walls have been excavated, and many interesting sculptured remains have been discovered.

The principal remains of the abbey consist of the north wall of the nave of the church. It has eight windows, the lights and tracery of which, alternately varied, are extremely beautiful.

The church has been 371 feet long and 60 broad. From the portions of it which yet remain, the west front must have been very beautiful; and the ornaments of the doorway are much admired. The bases of the pillars and walls of the choir may be seen, as may also those of the chapter-house. An old Norman arch, now the entrance to the Museum Gardens from Marygate, formed the principal entrance. In the Bootham portion of the wall, built by the monks to defend them from the assaults of the citizens, is a similar arch, and another near the Hospitium.

THE MUSEUM is an elegant Doric structure, erected in 1827. The collections in natural history and geology are extensive and arranged with systematic care. The museum belongs to the Yorkshire Philosophical Society. An *Ichthyosaurus Crassimanus*, 30 feet in length, found in the alum shale to the north of Whitby, is believed to be the largest tolerably perfect specimen of this gigantic fossil monster known. There is here also a *Plesiosaurus Zetlandicus*, from the lias of Lofthouse near Redcar, the only example known of this remarkable species. Among other objects deserving of attention here, is the interesting collection of bones of extinct British quadrupeds from Bielbeck's farm, near Market Weighton, including the lion, bison, rhinoceros, etc.; tibia of the mammoth, found at Pocklington; as well as a quantity of the bones found in the famous Kirkdale Cave. The *Theatre* contains the earliest known specimens of English Tapestry, 1578. Catalogues of the contents of the museum may be had on the spot.

THE HOSPITIUM, a singular building of stone and timber, in the lower part of the grounds, is supposed to have been erected for the accommodation of strangers who were not admitted to the principal apartments of the monastery. It has been restored, and is now used as a museum for antiquities. The Roman relics, in particular, are numerous and interesting, including statues, altars, tiles, urns, coffins, rings of silver, gold, bronze, etc.

THE MULTANGULAR TOWER, so named from its having ten sides, forming nine obtuse angles, is an object of very great interest to antiquarians. It is built of neat and regular courses of small squared blocks of stone, with five rows of red bricks as a "bond." There cannot be the slightest doubt that this is a Roman work; this point having been decisively settled by the discovery of Roman legionary inscriptions in the lower courses of the interior. It formed one of the angle towers in the walls of

Eburacum; a portion of which is still to be seen here, passing from the tower in a north-easterly direction. These remains of Roman work are in excellent preservation.

St. Leonard's Hospital, the ruins of which are on the right on entering the grounds, has been much more extensive than would appear from its present remains. It is said to have been originally founded by Athelstane, the Saxon, in 936. Through the favour of subsequent kings, and the rich grants it received from time to time, this hospital became one of the largest and best endowed foundations in the north of England. The present building was erected after the fire of 1137, which destroyed the former edifice. The existing remains are very interesting. They consist of the entrance passage, the ambulatory, and the chapel, a beautiful specimen of early English.

The Yorkshire Fine Art Institution (admission 1s.), with its fine arcaded portico, occupies the site formerly known as Bearpark's Gardens, opposite the De Grey Rooms, and near the Old Manor House. It was opened in May 1879, and there are summer and winter exhibitions of pictures and fine art objects in connection with it, as well as industrial collections every few years. The Exhibition Hall contains an orchestra and organ, and is used for concerts, etc.

Churches.—Many of these are of considerable antiquity. Taking them in alphabetical order, their principal features may be indicated :—

All Saints, North Street. This church is a mixture of the Decorated and Perpendicular styles. It has a fine spire and some good stained glass, which well repays the most careful inspection.

All Saints, Pavement, a modern edifice erected on the site of an ancient structure. In ancient times, says tradition, a lantern used to be suspended nightly on its tower, to guide travellers through the forest of Galtres. The present lantern tower is a very graceful erection. The pulpit bears the date 1634.

Christ Church, in King Square, has been recently restored. It stands on the site of the ancient Imperial Palace of Eboracum.

Holy Trinity, in Goodramgate, containing some curious stained glass, and several old monuments.

Holy Trinity, Micklegate, dilapidated and old, contains the remains of Dr. Burton. The foundation walls are of Roman masonry.

St. Crux, Pavement, with a brick tower, was built by Sir Christopher Wren, in 1697.

St. Dennis, in Walmgate, has a Norman doorway. The style of this church is a mixture of the Decorated and the Perpendicular. Henry, Earl of Northumberland, who fell at Towton Field, is said to be buried under a blue marble slab in the choir. There are several monuments, one bearing a female figure in the costume of the seventeenth century.

St. Helen, St. Helen's Square. This church has a handsome octagonal lantern tower, and a curious Norman font.

St. John, North Street, chiefly Perpendicular, and restored in 1850.

St. Margaret's, in Walmgate, is celebrated for its fine Norman porch, comprising four united circular arches, all curiously sculptured with figures, chiefly hieroglyphical. Drake is of opinion that this porch was brought from the dissolved hospital of Nicholas, without the neighbouring bar.

St. Martin-cum-Gregory, Micklegate, the tower of which is at the west end.

St. Martin-le-Grand, Coney Street, with some valuable stained glass, and an elaborate clock abutting at the east end.

St. Mary, the Elder, Bishophill, in the Early English and Decorated styles, with a good east window. The brick tower was built in 1659.

St. Mary, the Younger, Bishophill, has a square tower in the Saxon style. It is believed by some to be genuine Saxon work; but others are of opinion that it was reconstructed in later times.

St. Mary, Castlegate, is a pleasing structure of considerable antiquity. Its spire, 154 feet, is the highest in the city. It has been restored through the liberality of the late Dean Duncombe.

St. Maurice, Monkgate, a modern structure in the Decorated style, on the site of an ancient Perpendicular one.

St. Michael, Spurriergate, ancient, but mostly rebuilt. It has some good stained glass. The curfew bell is tolled in this church tower every evening at eight.

St. Michael-le-Belfrey, on the south-west side of the Minster yard, is the largest and most elegant church in the city. It derives its name from its contiguity to the bell towers of the cathedral. It was founded in 1066, but rebuilt in 1535, and is in the late Perpendicular style. Thomas Gent, printer, and author of numerous works connected with the topography and history of Yorkshire, is interred in this church.

St. Olave, Marygate, an ancient foundation, with some old

stained glass. Etty, the royal academician, is interred in the churchyard.

St. Paul, Holgate Lane, a new church, erected by subscription

St. Sampson, Church Street, rebuilt, except its tower, which is interesting, old, and shattered.

St. Saviour, a commodious edifice, mostly rebuilt.

St. Thomas, the Groves, a new church, of no interest.

There are numerous *Dissenting Chapels*, none of them, however, calling for mention, except the Roman Catholic Cathedral of St. Wilfrid, opened by Cardinal Wiseman in 1864.

YORK CASTLE, now become a gaol for debtors and malefactors, was once a noble and important fortress. Its walls inclose an area of four acres, and the castle-yard will contain 40,000 persons. As may be seen from our sketch of the history of the city, York Castle frequently was the scene of important events in former times. A fortress existed here long before the Conquest—indeed, the Britons seem to have had a fortified mound here before the Roman invasion. The fortress, of which some parts still remain, was built by William the Conqueror in 1068. It is probable that he found a Roman fortification on the spot, and replaced it with one more suited to his purpose. The only portion of the old castle of any consequence now remaining, is Clifford's Tower (order to visit required from Lord Mayor).

Clifford's Tower, so called from one of the first governors, is situated on a high artificial mound, and forms a picturesque and prominent object. It was the keep or donjon of the castle, and, with the rest of the fortification, seems to have been of great strength. In 1190 this tower was the scene of the self-immolation of upwards of 1000 Jews, who, in order to disappoint a bloodthirsty mob of citizens, destroyed themselves and their property by setting fire to the tower. When York surrendered to the Parliamentarians in 1644, the city was dismantled of all its garrisons except that of Clifford's Tower. In 1684, either by accident or design, the tower took fire, and the powder magazine blew up, reducing it to a mere shell, in which condition it has remained ever since. A strong wall surrounds the mound, to preserve so interesting a relic from further decay, and it was incorporated with the Castle domain in 1825.

The walls of the tower are from 9 to 10 feet thick. Its plan consists of four segments of circles joined, the largest diameter being 64 feet, and the shortest 45. The entrance is through a square building, which was added to strengthen it in 1642. Over the entrance are the Royal Arms, and those of the Cliffords. The interior of the tower is picturesquely clad with ivy and other creepers. In the centre of the area grows a large walnut tree, said to have been planted by George Fox, the founder of the Society of Friends, who was once imprisoned here. The summit of the tower may be reached by a staircase, and an extensive view obtained of the surrounding country.

CLIFFORD'S TOWER.

The other parts of the old castle were turned into a county prison shortly after they ceased to be occupied by a garrison. In 1708 they were pulled down, and the *Old Buildings*, now used as the *Debtor's Prison*, erected in their place. York Castle also includes the *County Assize Courts*, erected in 1777, and the *Felon's Prison*, erected in 1826. Enlarged and improved accommodation for prisoners has been recently made, with an entrance distinct from the one leading to the Law Courts and Clifford's Tower. A visiting order from the Home Office is necessary for admission. Everything is planned in the best manner for order and security. In one place may be seen the convicts, in their parti-coloured uniform, at work upon matting, etc.; in another, the debtors taking air and exercise in their open court. The different cells, from that of the ordinary culprit to that of the criminal condemned to death, are shewn; and, last of all, there is the ghastly collection of casts of the heads of noted murderers and other criminals who have been executed at York, and of weapons of all kinds with which the deeds of blood were committed. As a prison, York Castle has various interesting memories. In 1604, Walter Calverley, of Calverley Hall, the hero of the "Yorkshire Tragedy," was tried and executed within its walls. Here, in 1746, many unfortunate Jacobites were tried, and expiated with their lives their devotion to Prince Charlie. Here, too, in 1759, Eugene Aram, the murderer, whose name and story have been rendered immortal in the pages of romance and poetry, made his wonderful defence, which, though it could not save him from justice, elevated him above the vulgar crowd of criminals. Howard the philanthropist visited York Castle in 1787, and declared, after an examination of it, that it was the best regulated prison he had seen. Smollett has left a similar testimony in "Humphrey Clinker." In 1795 and 1796 James Montgomery the poet was confined here for newspaper articles which the government of the day regarded as libels. Here he composed his "Prison Amusements."

There are various other PUBLIC BUILDINGS deserving of notice in a survey of the city of York.

The Guildhall was erected in 1446 in connection with the Guild of St. Christopher, afterwards strengthened by the accession of the Guild of St. George. It was granted to the municipal authorities of the city on the Dissolution of the religious houses. The Hall is a grand old room, 96 feet long, 43 broad, and 29½ high. It is in the Perpendicular style, and is divided into a nave and aisles by two rows of octagonal oak pillars on stone bases, their capitals grotesquely carved. Most of the windows are filled with stained glass. The subjects are chiefly chosen from local history. The window commemorating the great banquet given to the late Prince Consort, in 1850, is well worth careful in-spection. The room contains a large painting by Richard Manders, of "Paul before Agrippa," a large bell captured at the storming of Rangoon, and one or two other objects of interest.

The Mansion-House, situated in front of the Guildhall, was erected in 1725, after a design by the third Earl of Burlington. It contains portraits of Kings William III., George II., George III. when Prince of Wales, the Marquis of Rockingham, etc.

The Assembly Rooms, in Blake Street, were erected in 1730 from the design and at the expense of the Earl of Burlington. Adjoining them is the Festival Concert Hall, erected in 1823. The Theatre, originally erected by Tate Wilkinson in 1765, has been within recent years refaced, at a cost of £3200, by the Corporation, who own the property. In Lendal Street are the handsome buildings of the Yorkshire Club and the new Post-Office. In St. George's Field there are swimming and other public baths.

THE CITY WALLS AND BARS.—The city walls existed before the time of Henry III., but the exact date of their foundation is unknown. They suffered much in the siege of 1644, but were repaired between twenty and thirty years after. In 1831, having fallen into great decay, their repair was commenced by public subscription, and carried on with considerable vigour. Large portions of these walls still remain in excellent preservation. The most complete and important part of the walls is that which lies to the west of the Ouse. It completely encompasses the city on this side, and forms a promenade, from which fine views of the Minster, Clifford's Tower, and other prominent buildings, may be obtained.

MICKLEGATE BAR is situated midway in this portion of the wall. This gateway is of great antiquity, and has even been attributed by Drake and Lord Burlington to the Romans—a point, however, on which they have been conclusively shewn to be mistaken. It seems to be generally agreed now that it is a Norman work. Previous to the destruction of its barbican, or outwork, the appearance of this bar must have been still more imposing than it is at present. It consists of a square tower built over a circular arch, with embattled turrets at the angles, each turret having a stone figure in a menacing attitude on the top. Above the gateway are the arms of Sir John Lister Kaye, Lord Mayor of York in 1737, with the inscription beneath, " Renovata A. D. MDCCXXVII." Higher up are the royal arms (old France and England, quarterly), between those of the city of York. Over each shield there is a small Gothic canopy. On the inner side of the bar are the royal arms again. It was on this gate that the heads of persons regarded as traitors were formerly exposed. Here the head of Richard Plantagenet was placed in 1460, along with those of other Yorkists, to be replaced the following year by the heads of the Earls of Devonshire and Wiltshire, and other leading men of the Lancastrian party. The last occasion on which human heads were exposed on this gate was in 1746, after the Jacobite rebellion.

MICKLEGATE BAR.

The oldest portion of the wall is that extending from Walmgate Bar easterly to the *Red Tower*, a curious old brick building, not much noticed. The wall is built on a series of rude and irregular arches, evidently of very great antiquity. On the portion of the wall extending westward from Walmgate Bar there is an agreeable public promenade.

Outside Micklegate Bar, on the left, is *the Nunnery*, a convent of nuns of the order of St. Ursula. This establishment is understood to be in a prosperous condition.

The Race Course is at Knavesmire, about a mile from York by the same road. It is an open plain, and is well adapted for the purpose. The Grand Stand was erected by subscription in 1754. The races take place in April and August, and are always largely and fashionably attended.

WALMGATE BAR is the only one which retains its barbican, and it is therefore a very interesting relic of antiquity. Walmgate is supposed to be a corruption from Watlingate; which is very probable, as the Watling Street of the Romans here entered. It is much in the same style as Micklegate and the other two bars, being square, with embattled turrets. The old door, wickets, and portcullis still remain. The arms are those of Henry V.

MONK BAR, so called after General Monk, is pronounced by Mr. Britton "the most perfect specimen of this sort of architecture in the kingdom." It is loftier than any of the other bars. The interior of it consists of two storeys of vaulted chambers, formerly used as prisons for freemen of the city. The portcullis is still in existence. The turrets are ornamented with small figures in the attitude of throwing down stones.

BOOTHAM BAR, the entrance from the north, is similar in form to the other bars. Its barbican, the most perfect in York, was taken down in 1831, but the bar remains.

BRIDGES.—Formerly there was only one bridge across the Ouse connecting Micklegate with the main part of the city. Two have been added—Lendal Bridge, a handsome single arched structure, forming a direct communication between the New Station and the Cathedral; and Skeldergate Bridge, near the Castle. There are five bridges over the Foss. The antiquated custom of charging tolls is still maintained on the Lendal and other bridges.

GENERAL DESCRIPTION
AND HISTORY OF THE COUNTY OF YORK.

YORKSHIRE is the largest county in England, exceeding by upwards of six hundred square miles the combined areas of Lincolnshire and Devonshire, which rank next to it in extent. In point of population it is inferior only to Lancashire and the metropolitan county of Middlesex. The outline is an irregular quadrangle, marked out by great natural boundaries. Its whole east side is washed by the German Ocean; on the north, the Tees separates it from Durham; on the south, the Humber divides it from Lincoln; while a range of hills on the west almost exactly defines its limits towards Westmorland and Lancashire.

The lands of Yorkshire slope to the east and south, in accordance with their internal structure. With only one or two slight exceptions, such as the "Whinstone Dike" and "Whin Sill," the mineral masses are regularly stratified; they are not, however, horizontal, but inclined to the eastward, receiving their axis of elevation from a great line of dislocation nearly coincident with the western boundary of the county. The surface of the county may be divided into distinctly-marked natural districts, each of which has superficial characteristics of scenery, as well as an internal formation, peculiarly its own. In the centre of the county, stretching from the Tees to the Humber, is the great Vale of York, a beautiful and fertile tract upon the New Red Sandstone series, bordered on the east by the Lias, and on the west by the

Gunnerside in Swaledale

Magnesian Limestone. The bold and picturesque scenery of the western hills and dales is due to the harder rocks of the Millstone Grit series and the Scar Limestone, which here come to the surface. In the south-western part of the county we have a considerable tract of the Coal formation, the site of the great manufacturing towns of the West Riding, and densely peopled throughout. The north-eastern district is of the Oolitic and Lias formations; and the south-eastern district, with its smooth green wolds, is of Chalk. Between these districts lies the Vale of Pickering, which in prehistoric times was either a river course or a lake opening to the sea. The formation of this tract is of Kimmeridge clay, covered by lacustrine and river deposits. In the portion of the south-eastern district, which is called Holderness, the chalk gives place to a perishable formation of sand, gravel, clay, and lake and river sediment, on which the sea makes constant and easy encroachments.

"The main external features of Yorkshire," says Professor Phillips, "are strictly explicable on the simplest possible theory: viz., that of the long continued action of the agitated sea on the strata which composed its bed, at the time when this bed was raised to constitute land. These strata, by their various degrees of consolidation and peculiarities of position, offered unequal resistance to the waves, and have been unequally wasted; the softer strata, which suffered most waste, have left the greatest hollows—the red marls and blue lias having been excavated in the Vale of York, the Kimmeridge clays in the Vale of Pickering, the limestone shales in Craven, and the tertiary sands in Holderness; while harder masses of chalk constitute the wolds, oolites and sandstones form the moorlands of Whitby, still firmer sandstones and limestones, with some slaty and some basaltic masses, constitute the higher regions of the west.

"To geological differences on a large scale we thus clearly trace the main distinctive features of the great natural divisions of Yorkshire. The mineral qualities and positions of rocks, with the accidents to which they have been subjected, give us the clue to the forms of mountains and valleys, the aspect of waterfalls and rocks, the prevalent herbage, and the agricultural appropriation. Even surface colour and pictorial effect are not fully understood without geological inquiry. While limestone 'scars' support a sweet green turf, and slopes of shale give a stunted growth of bluish sedge, gritstone 'edges' are often deeply covered by brown heath, and abandoned to grouse, the sportsman, or the peat-cutter. In a word, geological distinctions are nowhere more boldly marked than in Yorkshire, or more constantly in harmony with the other leading facts of physical geography."

Perhaps no county in England possesses such varied and interesting scenery, whether sea-coast or inland. From the lofty summits of Mickle Fell, Whernside, Ingleborough, and the other hills in the western range, down to the level and extensive Vale of York, and eastward to the chalk wolds over the Humber, the high moors above the Esk, and the indented sea-coast beyond, there is a succession of scenery presenting every order of beauty, from the wildest sublimity to the gentlest loveliness. The dales of Yorkshire are acknowledged to be unequalled by any others in the kingdom; and some of them, in the more remote parts of the county, present, both in their scenery and their inhabitants, attractions of no ordinary kind to the adventurous tourist.

The climate, like the soil, varies in different places. The western moors and dales have a bracing climate, the cold being more severe than on the eastern heights. The climate of the central part of the county is equable and healthy. The highest points are Mickle Fell, in the north-west angle of the county, 2600 feet above the sea; Whernside, 2384; Ingleborough, 2361; and other hills of rather less altitude in the west; and Burton Head, 1485, in the north-east. The waters of Yorkshire, with the exception of that very small part of the county on the west slope of the Pennine chain which is drained by the Ribble, all find their way to the eastern sea at points within the limits of the county. The principal rivers unite in the Humber. They are—the Don, Calder, Aire, Wharfe, Nid, Ure, Swale, Derwent, and Hull. The Esk has its own outfall to the sea, as has also the Tees, which forms the northern boundary of the county.

The earliest inhabitants of Yorkshire, of whom we have any record, were the Brigantes, one of the most powerful British tribes. Their territories appear to have included Yorkshire and Lancashire, with perhaps portions of the neighbouring counties. Cartismandua, who delivered up the heroic Caractacus to the Romans, A. D. 51, was queen of this tribe. This action probably conciliated the Romans for a time; for the Brigantes were not reduced under the power of that nation till the reign of

Vespasian, in the year 71. When Constantine divided Britain into three parts, Yorkshire was included in *Maxima Cæsariensis*. Under the Saxons it formed part of the kingdom of Northumberland, having the name of Deira, when that kingdom was divided into two parts. Along with the rest of the kingdom of Northumbria, Yorkshire yielded to Egbert, king of the West Saxons, about the year 827. On the invasion of the Danes, Yorkshire was reduced after some sanguinary conflicts, in one of which the rival Saxon kings, Osbert and Ella, too late in uniting against the common foe, were slain at York, in 867. Seventy years later, Athelstan " of earls the lord, of heroes the bracelet giver," defeated the Danes in a bloody battle, and brought Northumbria again under Saxon rule. Again and again the Danes renewed the contest, as their fleets landed fresh troops of hardy Northmen on the English coast. The last great struggle was fought in 1066. Hadrada, king of Norway, entered the Humber with 500 ships, and landed an army, which, with that of the Danish prince Tosti, who had invited him, amounted to 60,000 men. Marching upon York, the invaders speedily took it by storm. Harold, the Saxon king of England, at once marched towards York to oppose the invaders, who withdrew, and took up a strong position at Stamford Brig. The dauntless Harold at once attacked them. The battle raged from seven in the morning till three in the afternoon, and issued in the death of Hadrada and Tosti, and the almost total destruction of their army. Three weeks later, Harold had to resist another invader; and the " last of the Saxons " perished on the field of Hastings. William the Conqueror pursued the same policy towards Yorkshire as towards the rest of the kingdom. He garrisoned York, and bestowed the castles and manors throughout the county on his followers. Several risings against the Norman power, which took place in this county, were punished with great severity. The first parliament mentioned in history, was held in York, by Henry II., in 1160. Many of the principal facts in the history of the county after this period fall to be noticed in that of its chief city, which continued for a long period to be the scene of many of the most important events in our national history.
During the wars of the Roses, Yorkshire was the scene of various important struggles, the chief of which were the battles of Wakefield in 1460, and of Towton in 1461. The suppression of monastic houses by Henry VIII. gave

rise to a serious rebellion, commonly called the "Pilgrimage of Grace," in 1536. Several smaller risings occurred shortly after this period; but they were easily and summarily suppressed. Yorkshire was the theatre of many struggles between the royalists and parliamentarians. It was at Marston Moor that the important battle was fought which gave a blow to the fortunes of the haughty and unfortunate Charles, from which they never recovered. With the exception of some royal visits, and several risings in the manufacturing districts, occasioned by commercial distress and the introduction of machinery, the subsequent history of this county presents no events deserving special notice.

Yorkshire contains numerous remains of the peoples who have successively ruled it. The Brigantes or Highlanders—that being the meaning of their name—have left traces of themselves in the names of many of the rivers, and some of the mountains and ancient sites of population; in their tumuli, containing bones, weapons, and ornaments, to be seen on the Wolds and elsewhere; in their camps, such as antiquarians trace at Barwick in Elmet, Hutton Ambo, and Langton; in their stone monuments; and in their pottery.

The Romans have left very numerous and distinct memorials of themselves. Their military roads traverse the county in various directions. One great line enters Yorkshire near Bawtry, crosses the Don at Doncaster (*Danum*), the Aire at Castleford (*Legeolium*), and the Wharfe at Tadcaster (*Calcaria*), and reaches York (*Eboracum*), whence it passes in a north-westerly direction to Aldborough (*Isurium*), then to Catterick Bridge (*Cataractonium*), where it crosses the Swale, and passing still north, leaves the county by crossing the Tees at Pierse Bridge. A little to the north of Catterick, a branch of the road goes off to the left to Greta Bridge, whence it proceeds towards Carlisle. From Eboracum, a road in many places well marked goes eastward by *Derventio* (Malton) and *Delgovitia*, to *Praetorium* (Dunsley). From Isurium several lines of road branch off; one, very distinctly marked, proceeding in a south-westerly direction, crossing the Nid, Wharfe, and Aire, and following the course of the Ribble towards Preston. Roman camps are numerous. The earliest of their stations appears to have been at Aldborough. Traces, more or less distinct, may be seen of camps at York, Bainbridge, Catterick Bridge, Greta Bridge, Stainmoor, Malton, and Cawthorne; while the names and positions of numerous other places, taken in conjunction with the geography of Ptolemy and the itineraries of Antoninus, make it evident that they were Roman settlements. Relics of the Romans have been frequently found, in the shape of votive altars, stone coffins, pavements, sculptures, coins, ornaments of glass, coral, bronze, gold and silver, etc.*

The Anglo-Saxons and Danes are not without their monuments. These are chiefly mounds, raised either for defence or as memorials for the fallen brave. Warlike weapons and ornaments of various kinds have been found in these mounds. The remains of Saxon architecture which Yorkshire possesses consist chiefly of a few pillars, arches, and inscriptions, preserved by being incorporated with later structures. These, which are chiefly in churches, are very interesting. Norman remains are more numerous, and are to be found in much purity and perfection in various castles and ecclesiastical edifices. There are many old fortresses in this county, which are interesting alike for the antiquity of their erection and their historical associations. Its stately minsters, still preserved in their old magnificence, its ancient churches, and the grand ruins of its crumbling abbeys, present abundant and excellent materials for a study and comparison of the different orders of architecture.

This extensive county has given to the world many eminent names. The principal natives of Yorkshire who figure prominently in public affairs, in ancient times, are: Richard Plantagenet, third Duke of York, whose ambition and fate are

* EARLY INHABITANTS.—The researches in the tumuli of the wolds and moors, conducted through several years by the Rev. Canon Greenwell of Durham, and with him Sir John Lubbock, Bart. (author of *Pre-Historic Times*); John Evans, Esq., F.R.S., F.S.A., of Hemel Hempstead; Mr. Monkman, Malton; and the Rev. Fred. Porter, Yedingham, have shown that in prehistoric times two races of people inhabited Yorkshire. The earlier race (so thought) was peculiar for long heads (dolicho-cephalic), and buried in long barrows mostly, and had the plainest of pottery, and nothing but stone or flint weapons and implements. Another race, of round heads (brachy-cephalic), buried in round barrows, had a knowledge of metal, implements of bronze being found with their interments, along with ornate pottery and flint implements. The Rev. Canon Greenwell has published a work on the prehistoric people, under the title *A Decade of Skulls from Ancient Northumbria*. Recent excavations at Ulrome, near Driffield, have brought to light an extensive prehistoric lake-dwelling, with some implements of a previously unknown type.

celebrated by Shakspere in "King Henry VI.;" Richard Scroop, also immortalized by Shakspere, beheaded for high treason in 1405; John Fisher, Bishop of Rochester, and afterwards Cardinal, born in 1458, and beheaded, for his opposition to Henry VIII., in 1535; Sir William Gascoigne, the chief justice who committed Prince Henry to prison for contempt of court, born 1350, died 1413; Sir William de la Pole, founder of the powerful family of Suffolk—the character of the fourth Earl and first Duke of which family is delineated in "King Henry VI., Part II."—died 1356; Andrew Marvell, the friend of Milton, and the consistent and unswerving advocate of constitutional principles, born 1620, died 1678. In later times, Hull, the place which Andrew Marvell represented in Parliament, has given birth to William Wilberforce, the friend of the slave, and returned him as its representative. He was born in 1759, and died in 1833. Of noted commanders Yorkshire claims—Thomas, Lord Fairfax, the famous parliamentary general, born 1611, died 1671; Sir John Lawson, the celebrated admiral, died in action, after a brilliant career, 1665; Sir Martin Frobisher, knighted for his gallantry in an action with the Spaniards, and killed in an attack on Brest, 1594. Several noted travellers were born in this county: Armigel Waad, styled by Fuller, "the English Columbus," the first Englishman who set foot on the shores of America, died in 1568; Sir Thomas Herbert, who explored many parts of Asia and Africa, and published an account of his travels, was born in 1606, and died in 1682; and Captain James Cook, the circumnavigator of the globe, born 1728, killed by the savages at the Sandwich Islands, 1779.

In literature, Yorkshire presents a vast array of names. Alcuin, the most distinguished scholar of his age, and the friend of Charlemagne, was born about 735, and died 804. Other natives celebrated for their learning are—Roger Ascham, the tutor of Queen Elizabeth, died 1568; Sir Henry Saville, an accomplished Greek scholar, and the founder of two professorships at Oxford, born 1549, died 1622; Dr. Joseph Hill, editor of Schrevelius' Lexicon, born 1625, died 1707; Richard Bentley, the celebrated classical critic, born 1661, died 1742; John Potter, Archbishop of Canterbury, author of the "Antiquities of Greece," born 1674, died 1747; Dr. Conyers Middleton, author of the "Life of Cicero," "Letter from Rome," etc., born 1683, died 1750. Several natives of this county have taken a high place as topographical historians and antiquarians by their works upon different districts of it. The chief names are those of Roger Dodsworth (1585-1654), Ralph Thoresby (1658-1725), Thomas Gent (1691-1778), Dr. Burton (1697-1771), Francis Drake (died 1770), Dr. Young, Rev. J. Hunter, Rev. J. Graves, Rev. J. Tickell, T. Hinderwell, Rev. W. Eastmead, Rev. C. Wellbeloved, G. Poulson, Professor Phillips, John Browne, J. Walbran, etc.* In an enumeration of writers on divinity belonging to this county, an honoured place must be given to John de Wycliffe, "the Morning Star of the Reformation," and the translator of the Bible, born about 1324, died 1384; and to Miles Coverdale, the English reformer, born 1499, died 1580. More recent are— Matthew Pool, author of the "Synopsis Criticorum," a classic in biblical interpretation, born 1624, died 1679; John Tillotson, Archbishop of Canterbury, whose "Sermons" hold a high place among the literature of the pulpit, born 1630, died 1694; Joseph Bingham, author of the "Origines Ecclesiasticae," born 1668, died 1723; Beilby Porteous, Bishop of London, author of a "Life of Archbishop Slaker," and various works in theology, and of some elegant poems, born 1731, died 1808; Joseph Milner, author of a valuable "History of the Church of Christ," born 1744, died 1820; John Pye Smith, D.D., author of "The Scripture Testimony to the Messiah," and other works, born 1775, died 1850. Next let us notice the men of science:—John Smeaton, civil engineer, the architect of Eddystone Lighthouse, was born in 1724, and died in 1792; Joseph Priestley, author of numerous works on experimental philosophy and other subjects, born 1733, died 1804; John Ellerton Stocks, M.D., a noted botanist, born 1820, died 1854; Professor Sedgwick, of Cambridge University, author of "A Synopsis of the Classification of the Palæozoic Rocks," was born about the year 1786. Yorkshire has produced a fair number of poets, though none of them stand in the highest rank. We take the principal names, in the order of time: John Gower, called by Bale "poet laureate," and said to have been the instructor of Chaucer, was the author of various works, written, some in English, others in French and Latin, died in 1402; George Sandys, translator of Ovid's Metamorphoses— a work to which Pope declares that English poetry owes much,

* Dr. Thomas Whitaker, the Dugdale of Yorkshire, was not a native of the county, being born in Norfolk in 1759. One or two of the latest of the names enumerated above may also belong to other counties.

was born in 1577, and died in 1643; Edward Fairfax, the translator of Tasso, died in 1632; Sir Robert Stapleton, the translator of Juvenal and other classic poets, and author of some dramatic pieces, died in 1669; William Congreve, the dramatist, was born in 1669, and died in 1729; Sir Samuel Garth, author of "The Dispensary," and other poems, was born in 1671, and died in 1718; William Mason, best known by his dramatic poem of "Caractacus," and his biography of the poet Gray, was born in 1725, and died in 1797; Ebenezer Elliott, the "Corn-Law Rhymer," born 1781, died 1849; Herbert Knowles, best known by his exquisite "Lines written in the Churchyard of Richmond," died at the early age of nineteen, born 1797, died 1816; Monckton Milnes, M.P., author of "Memorials of a Tour in Greece," and three volumes of poems, born 1809. In other departments of literature are—David Hartley, author of "Observations on Man," born 1705, died 1757; John Foster, author of "Essays in a series of Letters," an "Essay on the Evils of Popular Ignorance," etc., born 1770, died 1839; the late Earl of Carlisle, author of a "Diary in Turkish and Greek Waters," born 1802; Edward Baines, M.P., author of a "History of the Cotton Manufacture," born 1806. Several names of novelists occur, all of them females: Mrs. Hofland, author of "The Son of a Genius," and numerous works for the young, born 1770, died 1844; the Brontës —Charlotte, author of "Jane Eyre," "Shirley," and "Vilette," born 1816, died 1855—Emily, author of "Wuthering Heights," born 1819, died 1848—and Agnes, author of "Agnes Grey," and "The Tenant of Wildfell Hall," born 1822, died 1849; Mrs. Gaskell, the biographer of Miss Brontë, and author of "Ruth," "North and South," and other works; Miss Pardoe, author of "The City of the Sultan," "The Romance of the Harem," and numerous other works. To Yorkshire belong the painters— Benjamin Wilson, who flourished about 1760; William Kent, born 1685, died 1748; John Jackson, born 1778, died 1831; William Etty, R.A., born 1787, died 1849; and W. P. Frith, born 1819; the sculptor, John Flaxman, born 1755, died 1826; the engraver, William Lodge, born 1649, died 1689; and the actor, Richard John Smith, of the Adelphi, born 1786, died 1855.

The area of Yorkshire is 6067 square miles, or 3,882,851 statute acres. The population, according to the census of 1861, amounted to 2,033,610, and at the subsequent censuses as follows:—

POPULATION OF YORKSHIRE.

Division.	Area in acres.	Pop. in 1871.	Pop. in 1881.	Persons to acre. 1871.	Persons to acre. 1881.
North Riding	1,361,664	293,278	346,260	0·22	0·25
East Riding	750,828	268,466	315,460	0·36	0·42
West Riding	1,768,380	1,830,815	2,175,314	1·03	1·23
City of York	1,979	43,796	49,530	22·13	25·03
Total of County	3,882,851	2,436,355	2,886,564	0·63	0·74

In 1881 the total number of males was 1,420,001, and of females 1,466,563—the males exceeding the females in the North Riding by 3534.

The county is divided into four parts—viz. the three *Ridings* and the *Ainsty* of York. For parliamentary purposes the West Riding is subdivided into three districts—East returning 6 members, North 5, and South 8. The North Riding returns 4 members, and the East Riding 3. Bradford returns 3 members, Dewsbury 1, Halifax 2, Huddersfield 1, Hull 3, Leeds 5, Middlesbrough 1, Pontefract 1, Scarborough 1, Sheffield 5, Wakefield 1, and York 2. The North Riding contains an area of 2128 square miles, or 1,361,664 acres, and 346,260 persons. The occupations are chiefly agricultural, but mines employ upwards of 8000 persons. The total number of members returned from this Riding is 8. The East Riding, taking along with it the city of York, has an area of 1176 square miles, or 752,807 acres, and a population of 364,990. In this part of the county the number of persons employed in agriculture is almost equal to that of those engaged in every kind of manufacture. Cotton and flax, engines and ships, are the chief manufactures. The total number of members returned by this division of the county is 5. The West Riding is the most important part of the county in point of manufactures and commerce. Its extent is 2763 square miles, or 1,768,380 acres; and its population, 2,175,314. This is the great seat of the woollen and iron manufactures, of which details are given under the principal towns where the manufactures are carried on.

Agriculture is in a medium state of improvement, but is regarded as not so advanced as in Northumberland and Lincolnshire. Yorkshire, however, is more a grazing than an agricultural county. Craven, and the upper parts of the West Riding generally, are purely pastoral, there being scarcely any arable land in cultivation in this Riding, except in the lower districts. In the East Riding and the lower parts of the North Riding there are considerable tracts of good arable ground. Farms are generally small, and let at high rents from year to year. The total number of farmers in Yorkshire, according to the census of 1881, was 27,647 ; of whom 25,232 were males, and 2215 females. Farm labourers were reckoned at 61,861; 58,738 being males, and 3123 females. All these figures show a marked decline in the last twenty years. Cattle are mostly of the short-horned breed ; but there are large numbers of long-horns, and many varieties produced by crosses of these two breeds. Sheep are numerous, and also of different breeds. Yorkshire has long been celebrated for its horses. Many of the most noted racers which have appeared on the turf were bred and trained in this county. The Cleveland bays are highly esteemed as carriage horses. Horses for agricultural and general purposes are bred in great numbers in this county ; and the horse fairs which are held here at stated times are frequented by dealers from all parts of the kingdom, as well as by foreigners.

The mineral productions of Yorkshire are—coal in abundance, iron, lead, copper, alum, slate, limestone (some of it equal, if not superior, to the Derbyshire marble), building stone, etc. There are very valuable mineral waters in various parts of the county. Those of Harrogate and Scarborough have been long celebrated, and are much resorted to.

The East Riding, though containing the important port of Hull, is chiefly dependent on agriculture, and on the attractions of the beautiful watering-places extending along the coast. Until 1850 the North Riding was even less famed for its manufacturing industry, but the discovery of the rich iron ores in the Cleveland and Hambleton districts wrought a complete transformation in its prospects. While mining villages have sprung up in all directions, the town and port of Middlesbrough has been created ; other towns have increased with almost unexampled rapidity ; and Redcar and Saltburn have developed into fashionable seaside resorts. The great centre of Yorkshire industry is, however, in the West Riding, the foundation of its prosperity being the coal and iron field stretching from Leeds on the north to Sheffield in the south. But while iron and steel are the staple industries of Sheffield, and are extensively manufactured in other towns, it is for its woollen and worsted manufactures that the West Riding is chiefly celebrated. The West Riding has almost a monopoly of the worsted manufactures of the United Kingdom. The manufacturing district may be said, roughly, to include the whole of Yorkshire south of the Aire from Leeds to Skipton. It is deeply indented by valleys which originally supplied abundance of water for the mills, but now this is largely supplemented by steam-worked machinery, for which the proximity of immense coal supplies is a great advantage.

Andrew Gill: I have collected early photographs and optical antiques for over forty years. I am a professional 'magic lantern' showman presenting lantern slide shows and giving talks on Victorian optical entertainments for museums, festivals, special interest groups and universities.

For information about magic lanterns and slides and to contact me, please visit my website **Magic Lantern World** at www.magiclanternist.com

I have published historical booklets and photo albums on the subjects below. They are available from amazon, some as printed books, some as e-books, many in both formats. To see them all and 'look inside', simply search for one of my titles, then click the 'Andrew Gill' link. Alternatively, go to the 'My photo-history booklets' page on my website (see above) and click on the link.

Historical travel guides
Jersey in 1921
Norwich in 1880
Doon the Watter
Liverpool in 1886
Nottingham in 1899
Bournemouth in 1914
Great Yarmouth in 1880
Victorian Walks in Surrey
The Way We Were: Bath
A Victorian Visit to Brighton
A Victorian Visit to Hastings
A Victorian Visit to Falmouth
Newcastle upon Tyne in 1903
Victorian and Edwardian York
The Way We Were: Llandudno
Doncaster: The Way We Were
Victorian and Edwardian Leeds

The Way We Were: Manchester
Victorian and Edwardian Bradford
Victorian and Edwardian Sheffield
A Victorian Visit to Fowey and Looe
A Victorian Visit to Peel, Isle of Man
The Way We Were: The Lake District
Lechlade to Oxford by Canoe in 1875
Guernsey, Sark and Alderney in 1921
East Devon through the Magic Lantern
The River Thames from Source to Sea
North Devon through the Magic Lantern
A Victorian Visit to Ramsey, Isle of Man
A Victorian Visit to Douglas, Isle of Man
Victorian Totnes through the Magic Lantern
Victorian Whitby through the Magic Lantern
Victorian London through the Magic Lantern
St. Ives through the Victorian Magic Lantern
Victorian Torquay through the Magic Lantern
Victorian Glasgow through the Magic Lantern
The Way We Were: Wakefield and Dewsbury
The Way We Were: Hebden Bridge to Halifax
Victorian Edinburgh through the Magic Lantern
Victorian Scarborough through the Magic Lantern
The Way We Were: Hull and the surrounding area
The Way We Were: Harrogate and Knaresborough
A Victorian Tour of North Wales: Rhyl to Llandudno
A Victorian Visit to Lewes and the surrounding area
The Isle of Man through the Victorian Magic Lantern
A Victorian Visit to Helston and the Lizard Peninsula
A Victorian Railway Journey from Plymouth to Padstow
A Victorian Visit to Barmouth and the Surrounding Area
A Victorian Visit to Malton, Pickering and Castle Howard
A Victorian Visit to Eastbourne and the surrounding area
A Victorian Visit to Aberystwyth and the Surrounding Area
A Victorian Visit to Castletown, Port St. Mary and Port Erin
Penzance and Newlyn through the Victorian Magic Lantern
A Victorian Journey to Snowdonia, Caernarfon and Pwllheli
Victorian Brixham and Dartmouth through the Magic Lantern
Victorian Plymouth and Devonport through the Magic Lantern
A Victorian Tour of North Wales: Conwy to Caernarfon via Anglesey
Staithes, Runswick and Robin Hood's Bay through the Magic Lantern
A Victorian Visit to Cornwall: Morwenstow to Tintagel via Kilkhampton, Bude, Boscastle and Bossiney
Dawlish, Teignmouth and Newton Abbot through the Victorian Magic Lantern

Other historical topics
Sarah Jane's Victorian Tour of Scotland
The River Tyne through the Magic Lantern
The 1907 Wrench Cinematograph Catalogue
Victorian Street Life through the Magic Lantern
The First World War through the Magic Lantern
Ballyclare May Fair through the Victorian Magic Lantern
The Story of Burnley's Trams through the Magic Lantern
The Franco-British 'White City' London Exhibition of 1908

The 1907 Wrench 'Optical and Science Lanterns' Catalogue
How They Built the Forth Railway Bridge: A Victorian Magic Lantern Show

Walking Books
Victorian Rossendale Walks
More Victorian Rossendale Walks
Victorian Walks on the Isle of Wight (Book 1)
Victorian Walks on the Isle of Wight (Book 2)
Victorian Rossendale Walks: The End of an Era

Historical photo albums (just photos)
The Way We Were: Suffolk
Norwich: The Way We Were
Sheffield: The Way We Were
The Way We Were: Somerset
Fife through the Magic Lantern
York through the Magic Lantern
Rossendale: The Way We Were
The Way We Were: Lincolnshire
The Way We Were: Cumberland
Burnley through the Magic Lantern
Oban to the Hebrides and St. Kilda
Tasmania through the Magic Lantern
New York through the Magic Lantern
Swaledale through the Magic Lantern
Llandudno through the Magic Lantern
Birmingham through the Magic Lantern
Penzance, Newlyn and the Isles of Scilly
Great Yarmouth through the Magic Lantern
Ancient Baalbec through the Magic Lantern
The Isle of Skye through the Magic Lantern
Ancient Palmyra through the Magic Lantern
The Kentish Coast from Whitstable to Hythe
New South Wales through the Magic Lantern
From Glasgow to Rothesay by paddle steamer
Victorian Childhood through the Magic Lantern
The Way We Were: Yorkshire Railway Stations
Southampton, Portsmouth and the Great Liners
Newcastle upon Tyne through the Magic Lantern
Egypt's Ancient Monuments through the Magic Lantern
The Way We Were: Birkenhead, Port Sunlight and the Wirral
Ancient Egypt, Baalbec and Palmyra through the Magic Lantern

Birmingham through the Magic Lantern
Ballyclare May Fa
through the Victor
Magic Lantern
Bournemouth in 1914
A travel guide and photographs from one hundred years ago
A Victorian Visit to Brighton
A Victorian Tour of North Wales: Conwy to Caernarfon via Anglesey
The Way We Were
Cumberland
Dawlish, Teignmouth and Newton Abbot through the Victorian Magic Lantern
Photographs from magic lantern slides and text from a Victorian travel guide
Fife through the Magic Lantern
Great Yarmouth through the Magic Lantern
Oban to the Hebride and St. Kilda
The Kentish Coast from Whitstable to Hythe
A Victorian Visit to Peel, Isle of Man
Victorian Walks on the Isle of Wight
Victorian Plymouth and Devonport through the Magic Lantern
Thirty five 'magic lantern' photos and text from an 1883 travel guide
Southampton, Portsmouth and the Great Liners
Staithes, Runswick and Robin Hood's Bay through the Magic Lantern
Photographs from 'magic lantern' slides and text from a Victorian travel guide
Victorian Street Life through the Magic Lantern
CLOTHING
The River Thames from Source to Sea
How They Built the Forth Railway Bridge